Give yourself a star when you've finished an activity.

Use these stickers on the puzzle in the middle of the book.

10 Minutes a Day
Spelling
for ages 5-7

This CGP book is bursting with quick
Spelling activities for children aged 5-7.

Plus, it's packed with colourful stickers so they'll have
fun while they're learning all the essential skills!

Contents

The 'ai' sound 2

The 'oi' sound 3

The long 'e' sound 4

The long 'i' sound 5

The long 'o' sound 6

The long 'oo' sound 7

The short 'oo' sound 8

The short 'e' sound 9

The 'ow' sound 10

The 'ur' sound 11

Words ending in 'a' and 'er' 12

The 'ar' sound 13

Words with 'or' and 'ore' 14

Words with 'aw' and 'au' 15

The 'air' sound 16

The 'ear' sound 17

The 'f' and 'w' sounds 18

The hard 'c' sound 19

Words ending in 'ff' and 'll' 20

Words ending in 'ss' and 'zz' 21

Words ending in the 'v' sound 22

Words ending in the 'nk' sound 23

Words ending in 'tch' and 'ch' ... 24

Adding 's' and 'es' 25

Adding 'ing', 'ed' and 'er' 26

Adding 'er' and 'est' 27

Adding 'un' at the start of words 28

Tricky words 29

Puzzle: Spaceman Sam's mission 30

Syllables 32

Compound words 33

Words ending in 'y' and 'ey' 34

Words ending in 'igh', 'ie' and 'y' 35

The short 'o' sound 36

The 'or' sound 37

The short 'u' sound 38

Words with 'er' and 'or' 39

The soft 'c' sound 40

The soft 'g' sound 41

The 'zh' sound 42

Silent 'k', 'g' and 'w' 43

Words ending in 'le', 'el', 'al' and 'il' 44

Words ending in 'tion' and 'sion' 45

Adding 'ing' and 'ed' after 'e' 46

Adding 'ing' and 'ed' after 'y' 47

Adding 'ing' and 'ed' 48

More adding 'er' and 'est' 49

Adding 'y' 50

Adding 'ly' 51

Adding 's' and 'es' after 'y' 52

Adding 'ment' and 'ful' 53

Adding 'less' and 'ness' 54

Homophones 55

Contractions 56

More tricky words 57

Answers 58

Published by CGP

Editors: Keith Blackhall, Mary Falkner, Nathan Mair

With thanks to Gareth Mitchell and James Summersgill for the proofreading.

With thanks to Laura Jakubowski for the copyright research.

ISBN: 978 1 83774 018 5

Printed by Elanders Ltd, Newcastle upon Tyne.

Graphics used on the cover and throughout the book © Educlips 2023
Cover design concept by emc design ltd.

Text, design, layout and original illustrations
© Coordination Group Publications Ltd. (CGP) 2023
All rights reserved.

CGP, Broughton House, Griffin Street,
Broughton-in-Furness, Cumbria, LA20 6HH

CGP c/o Elanders GmbH, Anton-Schmidt-Str. 15,
71332 Waiblingen, GERMANY
info@elanders-germany.com

Photocopying this book is not permitted, even if you have a CLA licence.
Extra copies are available from CGP with next day delivery • 0800 1712 712 • www.cgpbooks.co.uk

The 'ai' sound

How It Works

Draw lines to match each picture with the **correct spelling**.

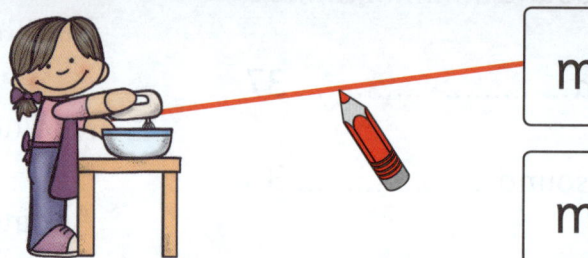

made
mayd

Now Try These

1.  rain / rayn

2.  say / sai

3.  playe / play

4.  trane / train

5.  plane / plain

6.  wai / way

7.  take / tayk

8. afraid / afrade

Good job! Give yourself a sticker.

The 'oi' sound

How It Works

Read each pair of words. Circle the word that is **spelt correctly**.

boi

Now Try These

1. toi / toy

2. point / poynt

3. coin / coyn

4. soil / soyl

5. noyse / noise

6. royal / roial

7. toilet / toylet

8. annoyed / annoied

Great work! Have a sticker.

The long 'e' sound

How It Works

Colour the picture next to the **correct spelling** in each question.

tree  trea

Now Try These

1. feed  fied

2. partie  party

3. feeld  field

4. silly  sillee

5. teepot  teapot

6. treat  trete

Well done! Find a sticker.

The long 'i' sound

How It Works

Look at the picture and read the sentences. Circle the **correct spelling** of the words in **bold**.

Susan and Jai **(like)** / **liek** snow.

Now Try These

1. Susan chose to **ride** / **ried** home.

2. Jai **cried** / **crighed** as he was scared of the dark.

3. Grandma was waiting for them with a **pigh** / **pie**.

4. The stars were **heigh** / **high** in the sky.

5. It was a cold winter's **niet** / **night**.

6. The moon was very **bright** / **brite**.

What a star! Give yourself a sticker.

The long 'o' sound

How It Works

Look at the pictures. Complete the missing word in each sentence using the letters in the box.

He walked along the r..oad..   a̶ o d̶

Now Try These

1. Flowers g............ in the park.   w o r

 2. They're in a b............   t a o

3. Jerry dug a h............   e o l

 4. We went h............   o e m

5. I scored a g............   a l o

 6. Sophie sp............ clearly.   e o k

Bravo! Choose a sticker.

The long 'oo' sound

How It Works

Circle 'yes' or 'no' to show whether each word is **spelt correctly**.

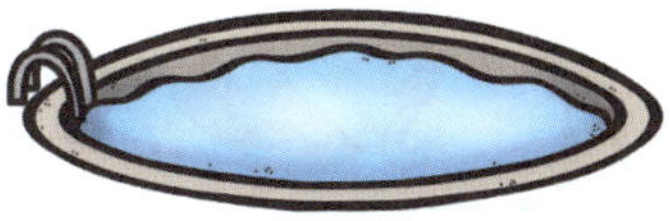

pool — **yes** / no

Now Try These

1.  fude — yes / no
2. 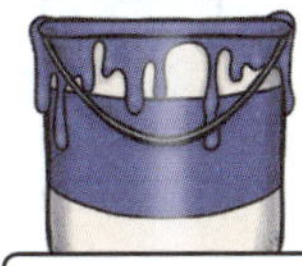 blue — yes / no
3.  flew — yes / no
4.  gewse — yes / no
5.  floot — yes / no
6.  threw — yes / no
7.  mewn — yes / no
8.  rude — yes / no

Cool! Give yourself a sticker.

The short 'oo' sound

How It Works

Read each pair of words. Tick the word that is **spelt correctly**.

hook	huk
	☐

Now Try These

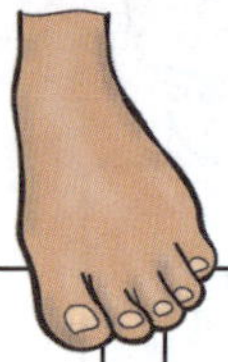

1. | fut | foot |
   |---|---|
   | ☐ | ☐ |

4. | hood | hud |
   |---|---|
   | ☐ | ☐ |

2. | bull | bool |
   |---|---|
   | ☐ | ☐ |

5. | wud | wood |
   |---|---|
   | ☐ | ☐ |

3. | cuk | cook |
   |---|---|
   | ☐ | ☐ |

6. | poosh | push |
   |---|---|
   | ☐ | ☐ |

Good job! Have a sticker.

The short 'e' sound

How It Works

Write '**e**' or '**ea**' to complete the words in **bold**. Each word should match the picture shown.

Paul **l**..ea..**nt** back in his chair.

Now Try These

1. Afnan goes to **b**..........**d** early.

2. I **r**..........**d** the newspaper yesterday.

3. The tools are in the garden **sh**..........**d**.

4. I want carrots **inst**..........**d** of peas.

5. Helen baked some **br**..........**d**.

6. Ahmed broke his pencil **l**..........**d**.

7. The spoon is **b**..........**nt**.

Excellent! Find yourself a sticker.

The 'ow' sound

How It Works

Read each sentence. Write the **correct spelling** of the missing word.

I live in a small ....town......

| town | toun |

Now Try These

1. Joe let the cat .... | owt | out |

2. .... do you clean the fish tank? | How | Hou |

3. My hamster is .... | broun | brown |

4. The goat ran .... the hill. | down | doun |

5. The dog is ready for his walk .... | nou | now |

6. The wheel spins .... | around | arownd |

Wow! Grab a sticker.

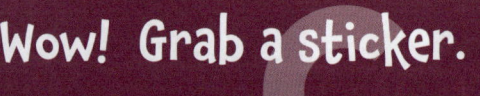

The 'ur' sound

How It Works

Circle the letters that are missing from each word. Each word should match the picture.

g__l   er   (ir)   ur

Now Try These

1.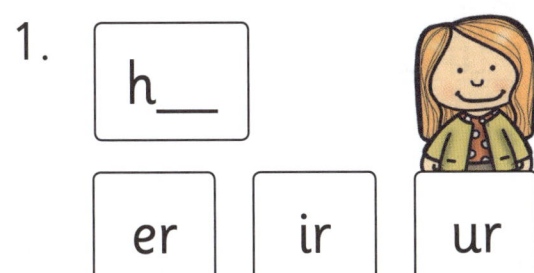
h__   er   ir   ur

2.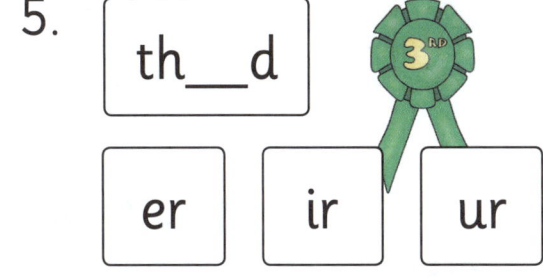
t__n   er   ir   ur

3.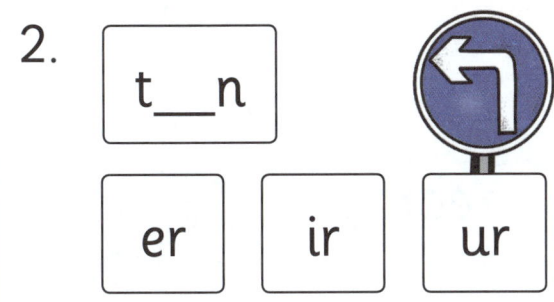
sh__t   er   ir   ur

4.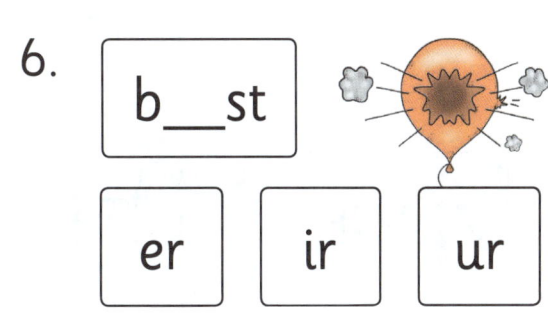
ch__ch   er   ir   ur

5.
th__d   er   ir   ur

6.
b__st   er   ir   ur

7.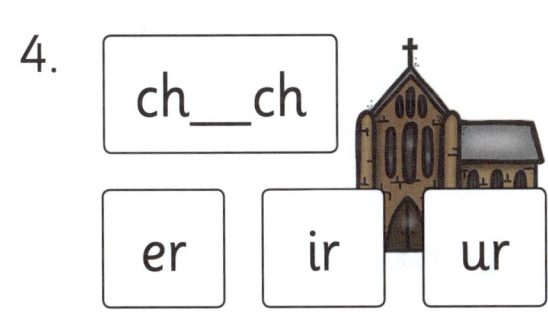
b__d   er   ir   ur

8.
p__son   er   ir   ur

Wonderful! Have a sticker.

Words ending in 'a' and 'er'

How It Works

Colour the picture next to the **correct spelling** in each question.

| summa |  | summer |  |

Now Try These

1. under    unda

2. sista    sister

3. zebrer    zebra

4. pasta    paster

5. deliva    deliver

6. camera    camerer

Super! Stick on a sticker.

The 'ar' sound

How It Works

Draw lines between the letters in each box to spell a word. The first letter of the word is red. Use the picture to help you.

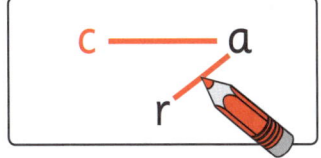

Now Try These

1. a m
   r
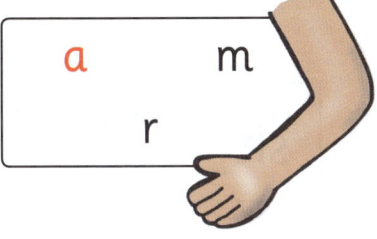

2. p k
   a r
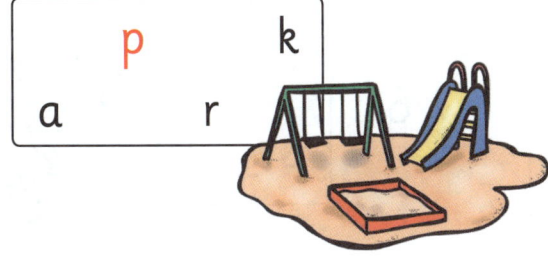

3. r f
   m a

4. r a
   s t
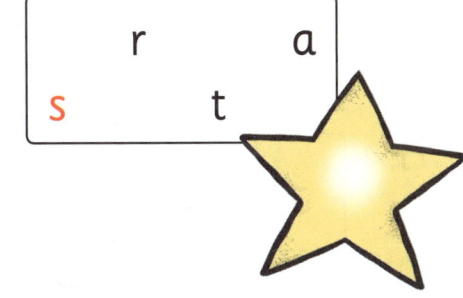

5. r d
   c a

6. s k
   h a r

7. g d n
   a r e

8. m a
   s r t
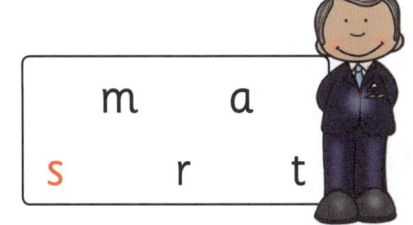

Nice work! Give yourself a sticker.

13

Words with 'or' and 'ore'

How It Works

Draw lines to match the words to the correct missing letters. Each word should match the picture shown.

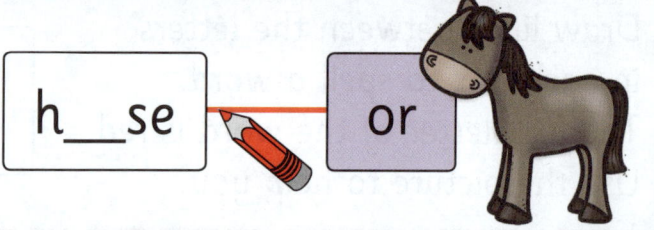

Now Try These

1.  sc__

2.  s__

3.  f__k

4.  t__n

or

ore

5. sh__

6. st__m

7. sh__ts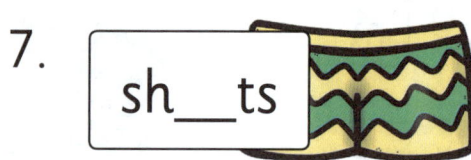

8. c__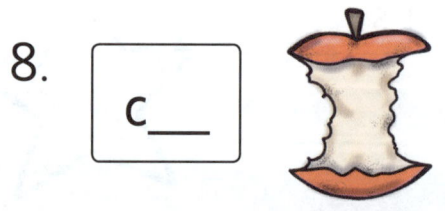

Good job! Find a sticker.

Words with 'aw' and 'au'

How It Works

Write '**aw**' or '**au**' to complete the words in **bold**. Each word should match the picture shown.

Tim is a famous ....au.....**thor**.

Now Try These

1. He is writing about a rocket **l**..........**nch**.

 2. The story is set in ....**tumn**.

3. The rocket takes off at **d**..........**n**.

 4. He needs someone to **dr**.......... the pictures.

5. His friend the **astron**..........**t** can't — she's on the Moon.

 6. His son can only **cr**..........**l**.

7. His dog can't hold a pencil in his **p**..........**s**.

Awesome! Give yourself a sticker.

The 'air' sound

How It Works

Read each sentence. Circle 'yes' or 'no' to show whether the word in **bold** is **spelt correctly**.

The **chare** is made of wood.

Now Try These

1. Leah **shared** her book.
   yes no

2. I ate a green **pear**.
   yes no

3. There's a **bair** in the cave.
   yes no

4. Wei saw a **fairy** today.
   yes no

5. I **ware** a uniform.
   yes no

6. Graham feels **scaired**.
   yes no

7. Tracey **cares** for other people.
   yes no

8. Bea is having a **haircut**.
   yes no

Great work! Give yourself a sticker.

The 'ear' sound

How It Works

Read each pair of sentences. Tick the sentence where the word in **bold** is **spelt correctly**.

Basma could **hear** music.
Basma could **heer** music.

Now Try These

1. It was **nearly** midnight. ☐
   It was **neerly** midnight. ☐

2. Basma **peared** at the sky to see the fireworks. ☐
   Basma **peered** at the sky to see the fireworks. ☐

3. The sky was completely **clear**. ☐
   The sky was completely **cleer**. ☐

4. The crowds were **chearing**. ☐
   The crowds were **cheering**. ☐

5. Basma shouted, "Happy new **year**!" ☐
   Basma shouted, "Happy new **yeer**!" ☐

Nice! Find yourself a sticker.

The 'f' and 'w' sounds

How It Works

Read each sentence. Circle the **correct spelling** of the missing word.

We _____ to the zoo.   whent   (went)

Now Try These

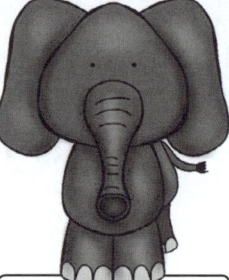

1. We saw a _____.   dolfin   dolphin

2. We wanted to see the _____.   elephant   elefant

3. There weren't any giant _____.   worms   whorms

4. My _____ loved the camels.   nephew   nefew

5. The seals had long _____.   whiskers   wiskers

6. The tigers lived in a big _____.   field   phield

Fantastic! Give yourself a sticker.

The hard 'c' sound

How It Works

Write '**c**', '**k**' or '**ck**' to complete the words in **bold**.

We made some ....c.....**akes**.

Now Try These

1. We went into the ....**itchen**.

2. Theo opened the **pa**.......... of butter.

3. Millie **cra**..........**ed** an egg.

4. She added **mil**.......... to the mix.

5. The syrup was really **sti**..........**y**.

6. I poured the batter into twenty cake ....**ases**.

7. The cakes cooked **qui**..........**ly** in the oven.

8. We let them ....**ool** before icing them.

Yum! Now find a sticker.

19

Words ending in 'ff' and 'll'

How It Works

Circle the letters that are missing from each word. Each word should match the picture shown.

we__ | ff | (ll)

Now Try These

1.  pu__ — ff / ll

2.  be__ — ff / ll

3.  cu__ — ff / ll

4.  do__ — ff / ll

5.  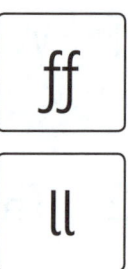 ti__ — ff / ll

6.   sni__ — ff / ll

7.   cli__ — ff / ll

8.  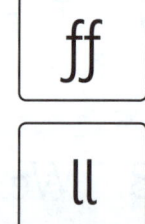 windmi__ — ff / ll

Well done! Give yourself a sticker.

Words ending in 'ss' and 'zz'

How It Works

Write '**ss**' or '**zz**' to complete the words in **bold**. Each word should match the picture shown.

Snakes **hi**......ss......

Now Try These

1. Raj and Mary are playing **che**..........

2. The bees **bu**.......... in the garden.

3. Windows are made of **gla**..........

4. I like listening to **ja**.......... music.

5. The monster is covered in **fu**..........

6. Dave is mowing the **gra**..........

7. The drinks **fi**.......... and pop.

8. The instrument is made of **bra**..........

You're the boss! Find a sticker.

Words ending in the 'v' sound

How It Works

Read each sentence. Circle the word in **bold** if it is **spelt correctly**. Underline it if it is **not** spelt correctly.

That's a big (**wave**).

I **lov** the sea.

Now Try These

1. Captain Charlotte is very **brav**.

2. The captain and her crew **live** on a ship.

3. The ship is about to **leav** the port.

4. They are heading for a secret **cave**.

5. They **hav** a lot of treasure on the ship.

6. They won't **givve** it to anyone.

7. To relax, the pirates like to **solve** puzzles.

8. When it's hot, they **dive** into the sea.

Brilliant! Give yourself a sticker.

Words ending in the 'nk' sound

How It Works

Look at the picture. Put a ✔ in the box if the word in **bold** is **spelt correctly** and a ✘ if it is **not** spelt correctly.

Do you **think** it will be icy?

Now Try These

1. Carl lives in a **pinck** house. ☐

2. Carl's house is next to the **bank**. ☐

3. Joy skipped by on her way to the ice **rinc**. ☐

4. Mia slipped on the ice and **sank** to the ground. ☐

5. Ije **dranck** some tasty hot chocolate. ☐

6. "Would you like a biscuit to **dunk**?" asked Tom. ☐

Nice work! Have a sticker.

Words ending in 'tch' and 'ch'

How It Works

Read each sentence, then circle the **correct spelling** of the word in **bold**.

My dog has a **patch** / **pach** around his eye.

Now Try These

1. My cat sometimes has fish for **lunch** / **luntch**.

2. I like to **watch** / **wach** my pets play.

3. The egg is about to **hach** / **hatch**.

4. The dog jumps to **cach** / **catch** the ball.

5. The puppy sits on a **bench** / **bentch**.

6. The rabbit will not leave its **hutch** / **huch**.

7. The hamster eats a **peach** / **peatch**.

8. The budgies **screech** / **screetch** loudly.

Purr-fect! Fetch a sticker.

Adding 's' and 'es'

How It Works

Draw lines to show whether the plural of each word ends in '**s**' or '**es**'.

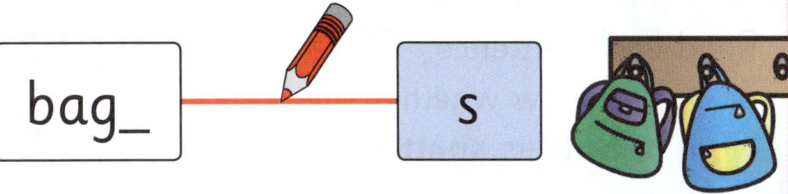

bag_ ——— s

Now Try These

1. pig_

5. match_

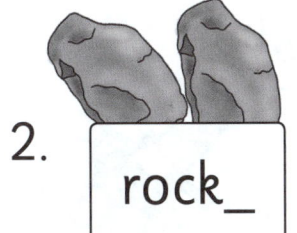
2. rock_

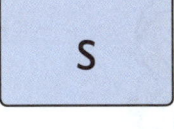
s

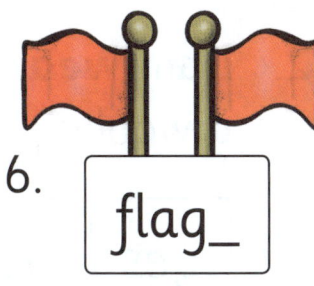
6. flag_

3. bus_

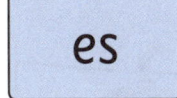
es

7. brush_

4. box_

8. van_

Awesome! Add a sticker.

Adding 'ing', 'ed' and 'er'

How It Works

Read each sentence. Circle 'yes' or 'no' to show whether the word in **bold** is **spelt correctly**.

 Jade is **eatting**. yes (no)

Now Try These

1. Daisy is a **paintter**.
   yes | no

2. I am **wearing** a woolly jumper.
   yes | no

3. Fatima **washed** her socks.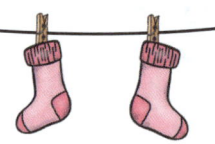
   yes | no

4. He is a science **teacher**.
   yes | no

5. He **borrowwed** her camera.
   yes | no

6. Gemma is **trying** to knit a scarf.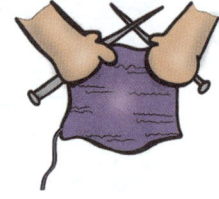
   yes | no

7. I **enjoyed** dancing at the party.
   yes | no

8. She is **aimming** at the target.
   yes | no

Great effort! Give yourself a sticker.

Adding 'er' and 'est'

How It Works

Read each pair of words. Tick the word that is **spelt correctly**.

 ✓ smallest ☐ smalest

Now Try These

1. ☐ softer
   ☐ softter

2. ☐ quickest
   ☐ quicest

3. ☐ shorter
   ☐ shortter

4. ☐ colddest
   ☐ coldest

5. ☐ slower
   ☐ slowwer

6. ☐ harddest
   ☐ hardest

7. ☐ depper
   ☐ deeper

8. ☐ sharpest
   ☐ sharppest

You're the best! Have a sticker.

Adding 'un' at the start of words

How It Works

Add the prefix '**un**' to the words in **bold** to complete the sentences.

Sukesh's garden gnomes are [**usual**] unusual.

Now Try These

1. They can be very [**helpful**] ....

2. They sneak around the garden [**noticed**] ....

3. They hide in long [**cut**] .... grass.

4. Sometimes, they [**plug**] .... Sukesh's lawnmower.

5. They often make the garden [**tidy**] ....

6. They occasionally leave the shed [**locked**] ....

7. The gnomes are never [**kind**] ....

Unbelievable! Stick on a sticker.

Tricky words

How It Works

Read the sentences. Look at the words in **bold**. Underline all the words that are **not** spelt correctly.

<u>Too</u>day, our **school** took us to the beach.

Now Try These

1. We **wer** excited for **our** day at the seaside.

2. Charlie **was** late, **soh** we left without him.

3. My **frend** took **some** food, but he ate it before we arrived.

4. When we got **thear**, we looked for shells **by** the water.

5. **Once** we had eaten lunch, I built a huge **sandcasle**.

6. Our teacher **sed** we could have **one** ice cream each.

7. **Tomorrow**, we will write about our **bisy** day at the beach.

Nice work! Find a sticker.

Spaceman Sam's mission

Spaceman Sam is on a mission to find alien life. Aliens only live on planets with correctly spelt words on them. Put a sticker next to all the words that are **spelt correctly** so that Sam knows which planets to visit.

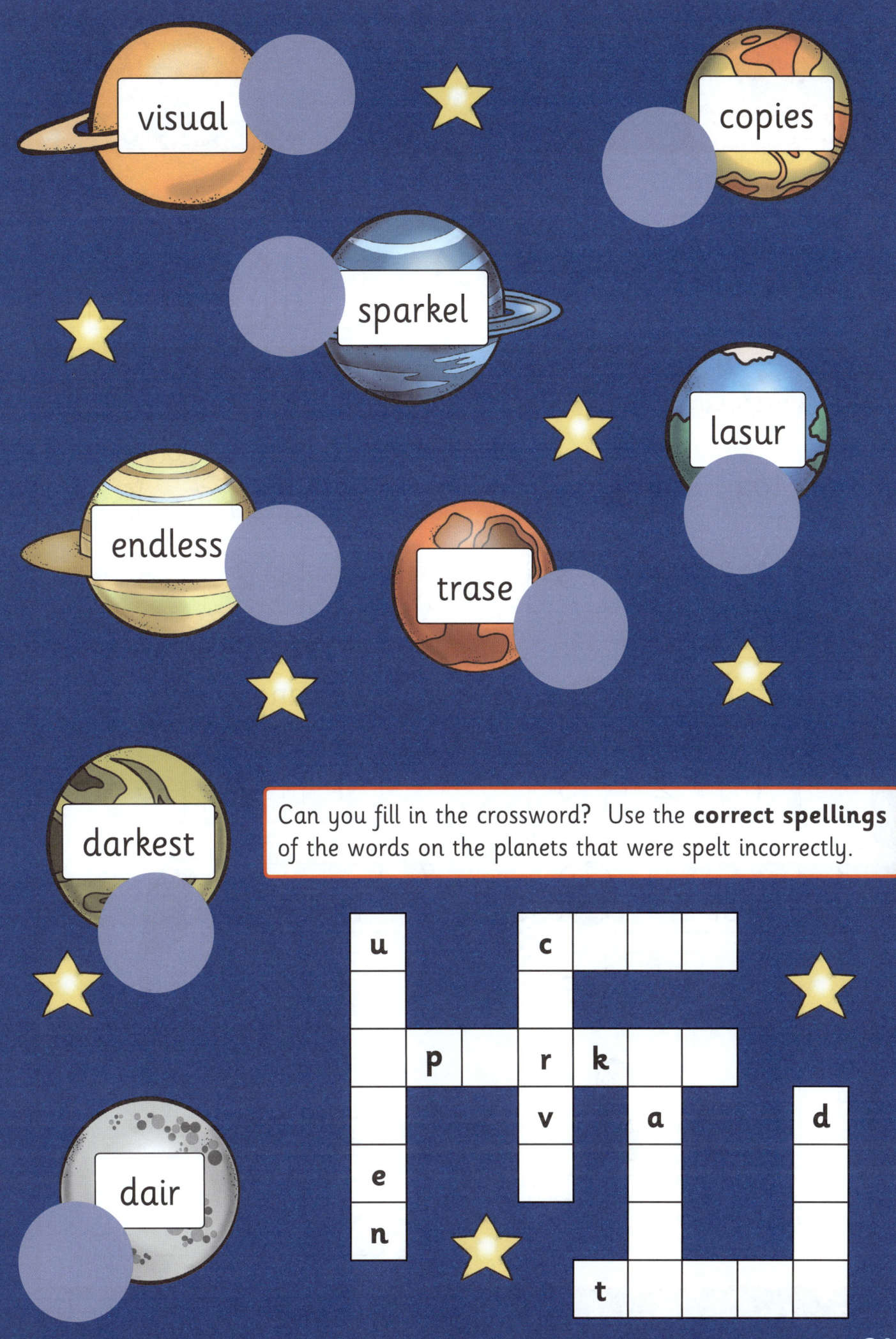

Syllables

How It Works

Look at the word. Circle the number of syllables that it has.

Now Try These

1. toy
   1   2   3

2. carrot
   1   2   3

3. lollypop
   1   2   3

4. draw
   1   2   3

5. summer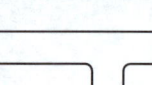
   1   2   3

6. volcano
   1   2   3

7. parrot
   1   2   3

8. gardener
   1   2   3

Good work! Grab a sticker.

Compound words

How It Works

Draw a line to finish the compound word. Each word should match the picture shown.

bed —— room

Now Try These

1.  back brush

2.  tooth berry

3.  snow flower

4.  sun pad

5.  note man

6.  blue pack

Great job! Pop a sticker here.

Words ending in 'y' and 'ey'

How It Works

Fill in the gap with '**y**' or '**ey**' to complete each word.

happ..y..

Now Try These

1. mon.......... 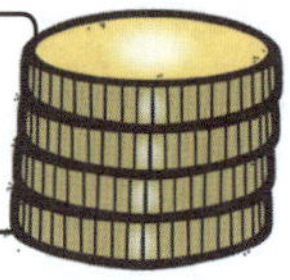
2. iv.......... 
3. donk.......... 
4. cherr.......... 
5. monk.......... 
6. fair.......... 
7. vall.......... 
8. sunn.......... 
9. hon.......... 
10. troll..........

Top work! Find yourself a sticker.

34

Words ending in 'igh', 'ie' and 'y'

How It Works

Read each sentence. Circle the letters missing from the word in **bold**.

Superheroes always **tr__** to help people.

[(y)] [ie] [igh]

Now Try These

1. This superhero can **fl__** .   [y] [ie] [igh]

2. She likes to be up in the **sk__** .   [y] [ie] [igh]

3. People **s__** with relief when she comes to their rescue.   [y] [ie] [igh]

4. This superhero wears a **t__** .   [y] [ie] [igh]

5. You can **rel__** on him to help people.   [y] [ie] [igh]

6. This superhero will never **l__** .   [y] [ie] [igh]

You're a hero! Take a sticker.

The short 'o' sound

How It Works

Draw lines to match the words to the correct missing letter. Each word should match the picture shown.

Now Try These

1. fr_gs

2. w_tch

   a

3. sh_cked

   o

4. b_ttles

5. squ_sh

6. sw_n

7. m_nster

8. squ_t

Well done! Give yourself a sticker.

The 'or' sound

How It Works

Look at the pictures. Circle the correct letters to complete each word.

w__ll — or / (a) / al

Now Try These

1. w__m — or / a / ar

2. h__n — ar / or / al

3. ch__k — al / a / or

4. c__k — al / or / a

5. sm__ll — or / ar / a

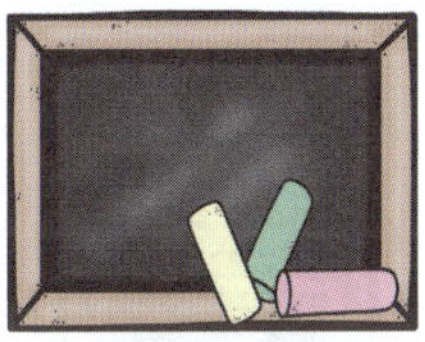

6. qu__ter — a / ar / or

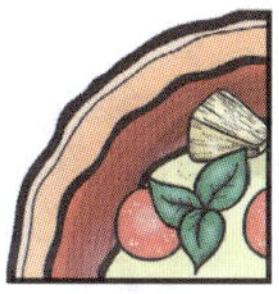

You're brilliant! Have a sticker.

37

The short 'u' sound

How It Works

Read each pair of words. Tick the word that is **spelt correctly**.

above ✓

abuve ☐

Now Try These

1.  some ☐ / sume ☐

2.  drum ☐ / drom ☐

3.  luve ☐ / love ☐

4.  jomp ☐ / jump ☐

5.  trock ☐ / truck ☐

6.  mother ☐ / muther ☐

7. 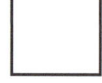 nuthing ☐ / nothing ☐

8.  uven ☐ / oven ☐

You're a star! Put a sticker here.

Words with 'er' and 'or'

How It Works

Look at the pictures. Fill in the gaps in the words with '**er**' or '**or**'.

w ..o.. ..r.. t h

Now Try These

1. w .... l d

2. s .... v e

3. w .... m

4. h .... d

5. g .... m

6. m .... m a i d

7. w .... k i n g

8. d e s s .... t

You're a winner! Have a sticker.

The soft 'c' sound

How It Works

Look at the picture. The sentences describe what is happening. Circle the **correct spelling** of the words in **bold**.

Now Try These

1. This park is in the middle of a **sity / city**.

2. There are some **mice / mise** hiding in the grass.

3. One **mouse / mouce** is eating some cheese.

4. There is a pink **houce / house** in the park.

5. Two children are riding **bicycles / bisycles**.

6. They are having a **rase / race** through the park.

Well done! Now, park a sticker here.

40

The soft 'g' sound

How It Works

Draw lines to match the words to the correct missing letter or letters.

 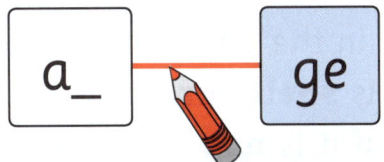

Now Try These

1.  bri__

dge

5. ma_ic

2.  __ar

g

6. villa_

3.  he_

j

7. in_ury

4.  _acket

ge

8. _iant

You're doing so well! Take a sticker.

The 'zh' sound

How It Works

Put a ✔ in the box if the word in **bold** is **spelt correctly**. Put a ✘ if it is **not** spelt correctly.

Glasses improve your **vision**.

Now Try These

1. Oliver has an **unuzual** pet.

2. Japan is a country in **Asia**.

3. It was a good **decijion** to bring a raincoat.

4. Pirates like to find **treasure**.

5. They **meassure** it carefully.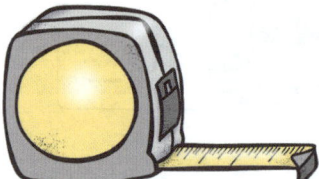

6. I go swimming at the **leishure** centre.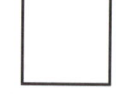

7. We like to wear **casual** clothes.

Nice job! Find a sticker.

Silent 'k', 'g' and 'w'

How It Works

Write the **correct spelling** of each word. Each word should match the picture shown.

| now | ....know........... |

Now Try These

1. | nome |

   ....

2. | nee |

   ....

3. | nat |

   ....

4. | riting |

   ....

5. | nock |

   ....

6. | not |

   ....

7. | rong |

   ....

8. | rapped |

   ....

Top work! Have a sticker.

Words ending in 'le', 'el', 'al' and 'il'

How It Works

Read each sentence. Fill in the gap with either '**le**', '**el**', '**al**' or '**il**'.

The joke made me **gigg**...le... .

Now Try These

1. I blew a big **bubb**...... .

2. The **squirr**...... has an acorn.

3. She has won a **med**...... .

4. Where is my red **penc**...... ?

5. My **tow**...... is blue.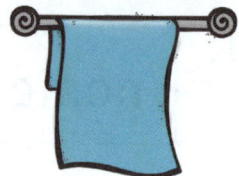

6. I work at a **hospit**...... .

7. I dug up a **foss**...... .

8. The blue hat is in the **midd**...... .

Put a sticker here. You're great!

Words ending in 'tion' and 'sion'

How It Works

Read each pair of words. Tick the word that is **spelt correctly**.

station

stasion

Now Try These

1. fiction
   ficsion

2. potion
   posion

3. causion
   caution

4. fraction
   fracsion

5. mantion
   mansion

6. location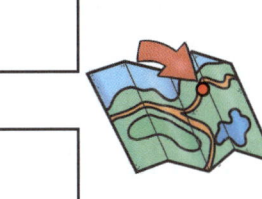
   locasion

Good job! Grab a sticker.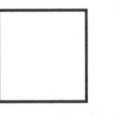

Adding 'ing' and 'ed' after 'e'

How It Works

Add the suffix (word ending) in the box to the word in **bold**. Write the new word on the line.

At lunchtime, Class 2B **decide** to play football. `ed` ......decided......

Now Try These

1. Arjun **race** off down the pitch with the ball. `ed` ....

2. Katie was **chase** after him. `ing` ....

3. The goalkeeper hadn't **notice** Arjun coming. `ed` ....

4. He was **wave** to his friend. `ing` ....

5. Arjun **score** a goal. `ed` ....

6. His team were **dance** around with joy! `ing` ....

GOOOOOAL! Take a sticker.

46

Adding 'ing' and 'ed' after 'y'

How It Works

Read each sentence. Circle the **correct spelling** of the missing word.

Lola and Zac were _____ to make a cake.

trieing | (trying)

Now Try These

1. Lola had been _____ the recipe very carefully.

   studieing | studying

2. She had _____ it into her notebook.

   copied | copyed

3. As she was _____ the mixture, she dropped it.

   carring | carrying

4. "Oh no, it's ruined!" Lola _____.

   cried | cryed

5. "Don't worry! We'll make another cake," Zac _____.

   replied | replyed

Nicely done! Put a sticker here.

Adding 'ing' and 'ed'

How It Works

Look at the word in the first box. Write the **correct spelling** of the word when the suffix in the second box is added to it.

......hopping......

Now Try These

1.  pat + ed

   ....

2. snow + ed

   ....

3. 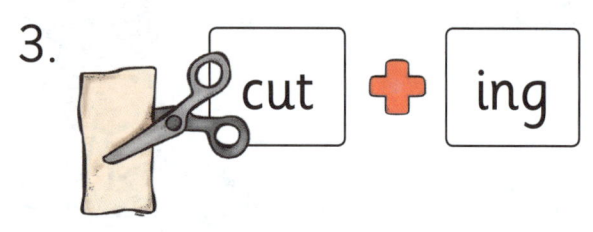 cut + ing

   ....

4.  drop + ed

   ....

5. sing + ing

   ....

6. mix + ed

   ....

7.  swim + ing

   ....

8.  dig + ing

   ....

Well done! You get a sticker.

More adding 'er' and 'est'

How It Works

Fill in the gap using the word in the box. The spelling of the word will need to change.

The spotty umbrella is ….bigg….**er**.

big

Now Try These

1. Yesterday was one of the ……………….**est** days of the year.

   hot

2. It is ……………….**er** to stay dry if you are wearing a raincoat.

   easy

3. We might see a rainbow ……………….**er**.

   late

4. Your wellies are the ……………….**est**.

   dirty

5. Tomorrow will probably be much ……………….**er** than today.

   wet

6. We had the ……………….**est** day playing in the snow!

   nice

You're the best! Have a sticker.

Adding 'y'

How It Works

Read each sentence. Circle the **correct spelling** of the word in **bold**.

Not all monsters are **scarey / (scary)**.

Now Try These

1. Some monsters are very **funy / funny**.

2. Monsters that are **slimy / slimmy** can be kind too.

3. Some woolly monsters make **yumy / yummy** sandwiches.

4. Pink monsters like eating **smelly / smely** cheese.

5. This **spotty / spotey** monster likes flowers.

6. This red monster likes to eat **juicey / juicy** lemons.

7. I think that **furey / furry** monsters are cute!

Well done! Pop a sticker here.

Adding 'ly'

How It Works

Add '**ly**' to the word in **bold**. Write the new word on the line.

Joel was sitting **quiet**.

..........quietly..........

Now Try These

1. He was **cheerful** reading a book. ....

2. A spider **slow** crept across the floor. ....

3. Joel **quick** jumped up. ....

4. "Help, it's a spider!" he shouted **loud**. ....

5. Miss Hatch walked over **calm**. ....

6. She **gentle** picked up the spider. ....

7. "Thanks Miss Hatch," Joel said **happy**. ....

You did brilliantly! Have a sticker.

Adding 's' and 'es' after 'y'

How It Works

Read each pair of words. Tick the word that is **spelt correctly**.

| berries |  |
| berrys | |

Now Try These

1.
   - dries ☐
   - dryes ☐

2.
   - babys ☐
   - babies ☐

3.
   - keys ☐
   - kies ☐

4.
   - trophys ☐
   - trophies ☐

5.
   - stories ☐
   - storys ☐

6.
   - turkies ☐
   - turkeys ☐

7.
   - traies ☐
   - trays ☐

8.
   - chimneys ☐
   - chimnies ☐

Put a sticker here. You're great!

Adding 'ment' and 'ful'

How It Works

Read each sentence. Circle the **correct spelling** of the word in **bold**.

Ruff the puppy is always full of **excitment** / **excitement**.

Now Try These

1. Yesterday, she was feeling very **playful** / **playfull**.

2. She chased a ball with great **enjoyment** / **enjoiment**.

3. She had an **argument** / **arguement** with Pickles the kitten.

4. "Be **carful** / **careful**!" Deji told them.

5. Deji took the ball in a swift **movement** / **movment**.

6. He was **thankfull** / **thankful** that this made them stop arguing.

7. It was **delighteful** / **delightful** when Ruff and Pickles fell asleep.

That was wonderful! Take a sticker.

Adding 'less' and 'ness'

How It Works

Look at the word in the first box. Write the **correct spelling** of the word when the suffix in the second box is added to it.

ill ➕ ness

............illness............

Now Try These

1. fear ➕ less

   ....

2. fit ➕ ness

   ....

3. kind ➕ ness

   ....

4. tidy ➕ ness

   ....

5. price ➕ less

   ....

6. lazy ➕ ness

   ....

7. care ➕ less

   ....

8. fuzzy ➕ ness

   ....

Amazing work! Give yourself a sticker.

Homophones

How It Works

Read each pair of sentences. Tick the sentence where the word in **bold** is **spelt correctly**.

The **sun** is hot.
The **son** is hot.

Now Try These

1. I see a butterfly over **there**. ☐
   I see a butterfly over **their**. ☐

2. It is nice and **quiet** in the garden. ☐
   It is nice and **quite** in the garden. ☐

3. I can only **here** the birds sing. ☐
   I can only **hear** the birds sing. ☐

4. A busy **bee** is collecting pollen. ☐
   A busy **be** is collecting pollen. ☐

5. I wiggle my **bear** toes in the grass. ☐
   I wiggle my **bare** toes in the grass. ☐
   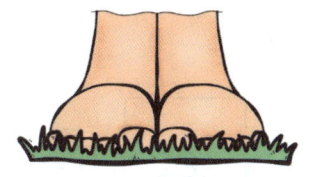
   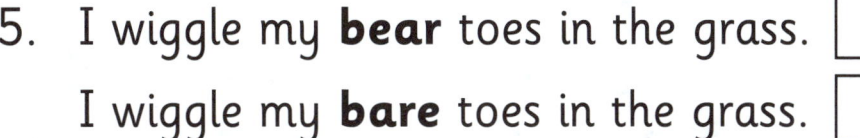

6. It is a bit **too** warm today! ☐
   It is a bit **to** warm today! ☐

You've won! Stick one sticker here.

Contractions

How It Works

Look at each pair of words. Circle the **correct spelling** of the words when they are added together.

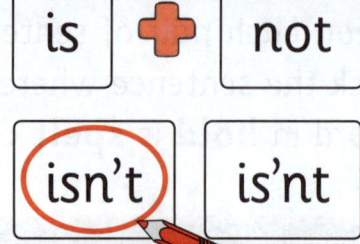

is + not

(isn't)   is'nt

Now Try These

1. it + is

   its'   it's

2. has + not

   has'nt   hasn't

3. let + us

   let's   lets's

4. could + not

   could'nt   couldn't

5. we + will

   we'l   we'll

6. they + are

   they're   the're

Tree-rific! Grab a sticker.

More tricky words

How It Works

Write the **correct spelling** of each word in **bold** to complete the crossword.

Now Try These

Across

3. I played tennis **arfter** lunch.
4. We **bowth** saw the goat.
5. Are you **shor** you don't mind?
7. I **cud** help you make the cake.
9. Many **peepul** like cats.
10. I **ownly** wear green socks.

Down

1. I drank a glass of **worter**.
2. We played inside **beecos** it was raining.
6. There is one toy for **evry** child.
8. **Hoo** is knocking on the door?

Put a sticker here. Great work!

Answers

Page 2 — The 'ai' sound

1. rain
2. say
3. play
4. train
5. plane
6. way
7. take
8. afraid

Page 3 — The 'oi' sound

1. toy
2. point
3. coin
4. soil
5. noise
6. royal
7. toilet
8. annoyed

Page 4 — The long 'e' sound

1. feed
2. party
3. field
4. silly
5. teapot
6. treat

Page 5 — The long 'i' sound

1. Susan chose to ride home.
2. Jai cried as he was scared of the dark.
3. Grandma was waiting for them with a pie.
4. The stars were high in the sky.
5. It was a cold winter's night.
6. The moon was very bright.

Page 6 — The long 'o' sound

1. Flowers grow in the park.
2. They're in a boat.
3. Jerry dug a hole.
4. We went home.
5. I scored a goal.
6. Sophie spoke clearly.

Page 7 — The long 'oo' sound

1. no
2. yes
3. yes
4. no
5. no
6. yes
7. no
8. yes

Page 8 — The short 'oo' sound

1. foot
2. bull
3. cook
4. hood
5. wood
6. push

Page 9 — The short 'e' sound

1. Afnan goes to bed early.
2. I read the newspaper yesterday.
3. The tools are in the garden shed.
4. I want carrots instead of peas.
5. Helen baked some bread.
6. Ahmed broke his pencil lead.
7. The spoon is bent.

Page 10 — The 'ow' sound

1. Joe let the cat out.
2. How do you clean the fish tank?
3. My hamster is brown.
4. The goat ran down the hill.
5. The dog is ready for his walk now.
6. The wheel spins around.

Page 11 — The 'ur' sound

1. her
2. turn
3. shirt
4. church
5. third
6. burst
7. bird
8. person

Page 12 — Words ending in 'a' and 'er'

1. under
2. sister
3. zebra
4. pasta
5. deliver
6. camera

Page 13 — The 'ar' sound

1.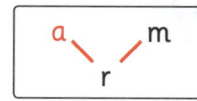
5.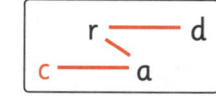
2.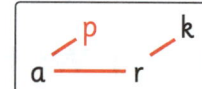
6.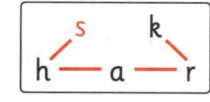
3.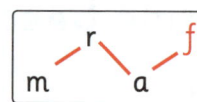
7.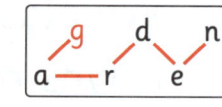
4.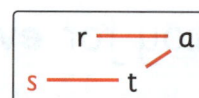
8.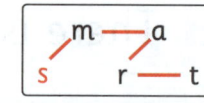

Answers

Page 14 — Words with 'or' and 'ore'

1. score
2. sore
3. fork
4. torn
5. shore
6. storm
7. shorts
8. core

Page 15 — Words with 'aw' and 'au'

1. He is writing about a rocket <u>launch</u>.
2. The story is set in <u>autumn</u>.
3. The rocket takes off at <u>dawn</u>.
4. He needs someone to <u>draw</u> the pictures.
5. His friend the <u>astronaut</u> can't — she's on the Moon.
6. His son can only <u>crawl</u>.
7. His dog can't hold a pencil in his <u>paws</u>.

Page 16 — The 'air' sound

1. yes
2. yes
3. no
4. yes
5. no
6. no
7. yes
8. yes

Page 17 — The 'ear' sound

1. It was <u>nearly</u> midnight.
2. Basma <u>peered</u> at the sky to see the fireworks.
3. The sky was completely <u>clear</u>.
4. The crowds were <u>cheering</u>.
5. Basma shouted, "Happy new <u>year</u>!"

Page 18 — The 'f' and 'w' sounds

1. We saw a <u>dolphin</u>.
2. We wanted to see the <u>elephant</u>.
3. There weren't any giant <u>worms</u>.
4. My <u>nephew</u> loved the camels.
5. The seals had long <u>whiskers</u>.
6. The tigers lived in a big <u>field</u>.

Page 19 — The hard 'c' sound

1. We went into the <u>kitchen</u>.
2. Theo opened the <u>pack</u> of butter.
3. Millie <u>cracked</u> an egg.
4. She added <u>milk</u> to the mix.
5. The syrup was really <u>sticky</u>.
6. I poured the batter into twenty cake <u>cases</u>.
7. The cakes cooked <u>quickly</u> in the oven.
8. We let them <u>cool</u> before icing them.

Page 20 — Words ending in 'ff' and 'll'

1. puff
2. bell
3. cuff
4. doll
5. till
6. sniff
7. cliff
8. windmill

Page 21 — Words ending in 'ss' and 'zz'

1. Raj and Mary are playing <u>chess</u>.
2. The bees <u>buzz</u> in the garden.
3. Windows are made of <u>glass</u>.
4. I like listening to <u>jazz</u> music.
5. The monster is covered in <u>fuzz</u>.
6. Dave is mowing the <u>grass</u>.
7. The drinks <u>fizz</u> and pop.
8. The instrument is made of <u>brass</u>.

Page 22 — Words ending in the 'v' sound

1. Captain Charlotte is very **brav**.
2. The captain and her crew (**live**) on a ship.
3. The ship is about to **leav** the port.
4. They are heading for a secret (**cave**).
5. They **hav** a lot of treasure on the ship.
6. They won't **givve** it to anyone.
7. To relax, the pirates like to (**solve**) puzzles.
8. When it's hot, they (**dive**) into the sea.

Page 23 — Words ending in the 'nk' sound

1. ✗
2. ✓
3. ✗
4. ✓
5. ✗
6. ✓

Page 24 — Words ending in 'tch' and 'ch'

1. My cat sometimes has fish for <u>lunch</u>.
2. I like to <u>watch</u> my pets play.
3. The egg is about to <u>hatch</u>.
4. The dog jumps to <u>catch</u> the ball.
5. The puppy sits on a <u>bench</u>.
6. The rabbit will not leave its <u>hutch</u>.
7. The hamster eats a <u>peach</u>.
8. The budgies <u>screech</u> loudly.

Answers

Page 25 — Adding 's' and 'es'

1. pigs
2. rocks
3. buses
4. boxes
5. matches
6. flags
7. brushes
8. vans

Page 26 — Adding 'ing', 'ed' and 'er'

1. no
2. yes
3. yes
4. yes
5. no
6. yes
7. yes
8. no

Page 27 — Adding 'er' and 'est'

1. softer
2. quickest
3. shorter
4. coldest
5. slower
6. hardest
7. deeper
8. sharpest

Page 28 — Adding 'un' at the start of words

1. They can be very unhelpful.
2. They sneak around the garden unnoticed.
3. They hide in long uncut grass.
4. Sometimes, they unplug Sukesh's lawnmower.
5. They often make the garden untidy.
6. They occasionally leave the shed unlocked.
7. The gnomes are never unkind.

Page 29 — Tricky words

1. We wer excited for our day at the seaside.
2. Charlie was late, soh we left without him.
3. My frend took some food, but he ate it before we arrived.
4. When we got thear, we looked for shells by the water.
5. Once we had eaten lunch, I built a huge sandcasle.
6. Our teacher sed we could have one ice cream each.
7. Tomorrow, we will write about our bisy day at the beach.

Pages 30-31 — Spaceman Sam's mission

You should have put a sticker next to: journey, flying, photo, moons, allow, action, visual, copies, endless, darkest

(crossword with words: crew, sparkle, unseen, pave, ease, dare, trace)

Page 32 — Syllables

1. 1
2. 2
3. 3
4. 1
5. 2
6. 3
7. 2
8. 3

Page 33 — Compound words

1. backpack
2. toothbrush
3. snowman
4. sunflower
5. notepad
6. blueberry

Page 34 — Words ending in 'y' and 'ey'

1. money
2. ivy
3. donkey
4. cherry
5. monkey
6. fairy
7. valley
8. sunny
9. honey
10. trolley

Page 35 — Words ending in 'igh', 'ie' and 'y'

1. This superhero can fly.
2. She likes to be up in the sky.
3. People sigh with relief when she comes to their rescue.
4. This superhero wears a tie.
5. You can rely on him to help people.
6. This superhero will never lie.

Page 36 — The short 'o' sound

1. frogs
2. watch
3. shocked
4. bottles
5. squash
6. swan
7. monster
8. squat

Answers

Page 37 — The 'or' sound

1. warm
2. horn
3. chalk
4. cork
5. small
6. quarter

Page 38 — The short 'u' sound

1. some
2. drum
3. love
4. jump
5. truck
6. mother
7. nothing
8. oven

Page 39 — Words with 'er' and 'or'

1. world
2. serve
3. worm
4. herd
5. germ
6. mermaid
7. working
8. dessert

Page 40 — The soft 'c' sound

1. This park is in the middle of a <u>city</u>.
2. There are some <u>mice</u> hiding in the grass.
3. One <u>mouse</u> is eating some cheese.
4. There is a pink <u>house</u> in the park.
5. Two children are riding <u>bicycles</u>.
6. They are having a <u>race</u> through the park.

Page 41 — The soft 'g' sound

1. bridge
2. jar
3. hedge
4. jacket
5. magic
6. village
7. injury
8. giant

Page 42 — The 'zh' sound

1. ✗
2. ✓
3. ✗
4. ✓
5. ✗
6. ✗
7. ✓

Page 43 — Silent 'k', 'g' and 'w'

1. gnome
2. knee
3. gnat
4. writing
5. knock
6. knot
7. wrong
8. wrapped

Page 44 — Words ending in 'le', 'el', 'al' and 'il'

1. I blew a big <u>bubble</u>.
2. The <u>squirrel</u> has an acorn.
3. She has won a <u>medal</u>.
4. Where is my red <u>pencil</u>?
5. My <u>towel</u> is blue.
6. I work at a <u>hospital</u>.
7. I dug up a <u>fossil</u>.
8. The blue hat is in the <u>middle</u>.

Page 45 — Words ending in 'tion' and 'sion'

1. fiction
2. potion
3. caution
4. fraction
5. mansion
6. location

Page 46 — Adding 'ing' and 'ed' after 'e'

1. raced
2. chasing
3. noticed
4. waving
5. scored
6. dancing

Page 47 — Adding 'ing' and 'ed' after 'y'

1. Lola had been <u>studying</u> the recipe very carefully.
2. She had <u>copied</u> it into her notebook.
3. As she was <u>carrying</u> the mixture, she dropped it.
4. "Oh no, it's ruined!" Lola <u>cried</u>.
5. "Don't worry! We'll make another cake," Zac <u>replied</u>.

Page 48 — Adding 'ing' and 'ed'

1. patted
2. snowed
3. cutting
4. dropped
5. singing
6. mixed
7. swimming
8. digging

Page 49 — More adding 'er' and 'est'

1. Yesterday was one of the <u>hottest</u> days of the year.
2. It is <u>easier</u> to stay dry if you are wearing a raincoat.
3. We might see a rainbow <u>later</u>.
4. Your wellies are the <u>dirtiest</u>.
5. Tomorrow will probably be much <u>wetter</u> than today.
6. We had the <u>nicest</u> day playing in the snow!

Answers

Page 50 — Adding 'y'

1. Some monsters are very <u>funny</u>.
2. Monsters that are <u>slimy</u> can be kind too.
3. Some woolly monsters make <u>yummy</u> sandwiches.
4. Pink monsters like eating <u>smelly</u> cheese.
5. This <u>spotty</u> monster likes flowers.
6. This red monster likes to eat <u>juicy</u> lemons.
7. I think that <u>furry</u> monsters are cute!

Page 51 — Adding 'ly'

1. cheerfully
2. slowly
3. quickly
4. loudly
5. calmly
6. gently
7. happily

Page 52 — Adding 's' and 'es' after 'y'

1. dries
2. babies
3. keys
4. trophies
5. stories
6. turkeys
7. trays
8. chimneys

Page 53 — Adding 'ment' and 'ful'

1. Yesterday, she was feeling very <u>playful</u>.
2. She chased a ball with great <u>enjoyment</u>.
3. She had an <u>argument</u> with Pickles the kitten.
4. "Be <u>careful</u>!" Deji told them.
5. Deji took the ball in a swift <u>movement</u>.
6. He was <u>thankful</u> that this made them stop arguing.
7. It was <u>delightful</u> when Ruff and Pickles fell asleep.

Page 54 — Adding 'less' and 'ness'

1. fearless
2. fitness
3. kindness
4. tidiness
5. priceless
6. laziness
7. careless
8. fuzziness

Page 55 — Homophones

1. I see a butterfly over <u>there</u>.
2. It is nice and <u>quiet</u> in the garden.
3. I can only <u>hear</u> the birds sing.
4. A busy <u>bee</u> is collecting pollen.
5. I wiggle my <u>bare</u> toes in the grass.
6. It is a bit <u>too</u> warm today!

Page 56 — Contractions

1. it's
2. hasn't
3. let's
4. couldn't
5. we'll
6. they're

Page 57 — More tricky words

Across: 3. after, 4. both, 5. sure, 7. could, 9. people, 10. only

Down: 1. was, 2. because, 4. believe, 6. even, 7. clouds, 8. who, 9. pryer

Give yourself a star when you've finished an activity.

Use these stickers on the puzzle in the middle of the book.